Circe

1.99

12/12

Circe

Nicelle Davis
Illustrations by Cheryl Gross

CIRCE

Illustrations: Cheryl Gross
Cover design: Alexis Vergalla
Book design: Dani Jean Keinz

Published by Lowbrow Press
www.lowbrowpress.com

ISBN 978-0-9829553-4-5

For J.J.

Contents

Book I: Sing to Me of Twists and Turns

Book II: In the One-Eyed Cave

Book III: Voices across the Air

Book IV: *The Recipe for Sirens*

Book V: Written in the Margins of *The Recipe for Sirens*

Book VI: Denouement

Book VII: Postscript

Circe

THE SAD SIREN

Book I: Sing to Me of Twists and Turns

First Time I Read The Odyssey *I was seven, gluing feathers to my arms, and suckling chicken bones to understand operations of blame. There was never enough about the Sirens. Using a word search, I found monsters' faults are not their own, rather products of another's story. Our county was small, but books could be shipped. I'd wait and wait to discover the accident of fish hearts pumping fast as bird's pulse—hunger is a half-cast spell—books end, and then all one can do is want more.*

Circe after Odysseus Leaves

What used to be a box of love letters
is now a book of spells. I read them.

They make me. Remake me. What
was, will be again. Page one. Again.

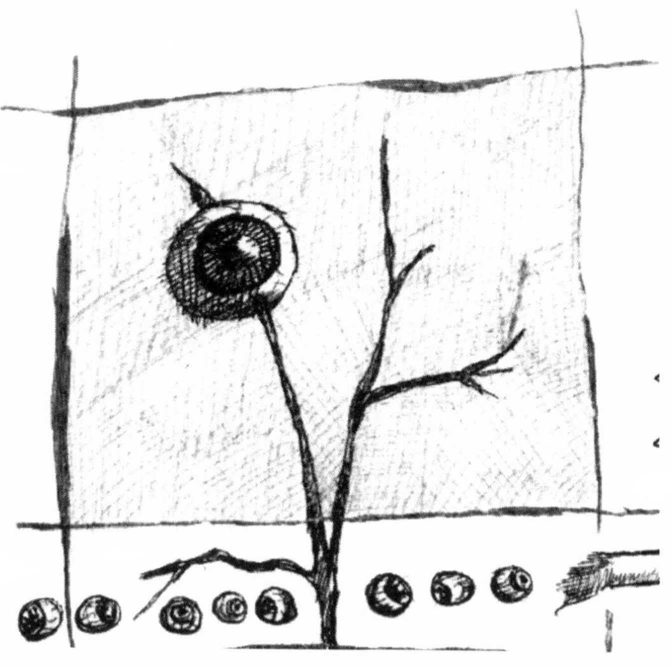

Book II: In the One-Eyed Cave

A Doctor Comes to Call on Circe

Do you remember me? he asks. I don't

feel like answering.

Patching my wrists like a weaver—
his hands look like spiders—

*You once gave me something, do you
remember?*

*I've given many things,
but remember nothing,* I say.

*You kissed my broken leg—promised me
it would heal.*

Did it heal?

It healed, but not the same.

Nothing can be recalled
in sequence. *You could be my son?*
I want him to know—

how proud I am to see his
hands move with even
kindness. My son….

Will we heal? I ask.

I can only stitch flesh, he replies.

Visions of Return from the Crystal Ball of Circe's Glass Eye

Odysseus exaggerates. Understandably. It is
broken cupboards and the scurry of unwanted
feet in walls—not mermaids—that make
walking away from the sea difficult. There was
song. That much is true. But that isn't enough
answer for Penelope when she's in a mood

for truth. She holds their son like a knife over
sliced figs—licks salt from the blade—
mumbles over its sharp edge, *Late night?* Yes,
he replies. The exchange ends with blue-
berries added to a dinner salad. Lemon juice
squeezed from the rind—the sun weeps from

her fingertips onto his plate of fresh greens.
Fish grilling. They talk about the possibility
of *digging up* the yard—purchasing top soil.
Making it all look *just a little better* than before.
Still there is a cupboard to fix, an exterminator
to call. *Can't risk depreciation. Not in this market.*

Circe Wakes Alone

Pigs are gone, but their shit's still here.
The well overflowed with last night's
rain, washing the floor of empty stalls
onto my doorstep.

I shovel with a makeshift spade—a jar
fastened to a branch—proud invention.
I work, happy with purpose, until I see
a man waving towards me.

Hands stained with dung, I wave back.
Then I notice he's with another woman.
Funny, however small a heartbreak,
it finds its way to

the deeper wound. Who is this man, other
than accidental kindness? Yet, when he
spoke, didn't it feel like homecoming—
Odysseus washed

again upon my shores? Pig's gone,
but I continue to shovel.

On the Day Circe's Only Friend Dies

I use a baby-basket to carry pomegranates to the blind woman—she is the last person in town who will see me. I feed her with my hands, little red wombs. There was a time she could tell me stories, but words have left her. Now I talk as though a book were written on my tongue—find myself weeping at the things I say—*Odysseus twofold. Lost lover. Lost son*—and find my friend asleep under the storm of my face.

I leave with my empty basket. Near home, a man walks onto his yard. From the looks of him, he'll call me *whore*. When I was *Circe*, I would have thought him handsome. I look to the ground for comfort—think, *my friend is not sleeping—she is dead—I must let someone know before dogs go for her bones.* I ready for the impact of stones as his mouth opens to the shape of a rock—

Hello neighbor, he says—

                and I nearly fall in a ditch—

I didn't mean to scare you, he says through links in the fence—reaching to help me, while fumbling a bottle.

                Don't, I yell—

I'm sorry he says—

                and it is all I can do to keep the sky stitched together

                You're not from here, I manage.

I'm from the East—visiting my sister, he says, *I was about to feed this piglet—neurological issues with this one—his mother ate his feet—you know, nature—but with some care, he'll be alright.*

All right, I repeat after him—

You alll right friend? he asks

and thunder follows. The sky's come undone,
I drop my basket and bolt for home—crying
like a baby's bottle in a footless pig's mouth.

A Love Letter for Circe

I nearly forget him, until a letter is pinned
to my front door with a knife—

ever speak to him
again
I'll cut off your tongue
and feed it to our pigs

Not the friendliest note, yet it feels good
to be addressed.

I make a game of the letter at breakfast—
jigsaw—

To your tongue,

speak to him again

and feed off our pigs

and I'll cut…

With the Festival of Poseidon nearly here,
imagine—

I'll…
…cast tongues in fire…tongues of fire…

The last man I kissed was Odysseus. Crying—
I swallowed the salt of us—loving the idea
of living by the sea.

Silly mouth games. Breaking apart only to come
back together. I admit. I never stopped
loving. Jigsaws.

Circe Dreams of Touch

I'm in a pigpen as he draws a bath.
Thrashing, I bury
my lower body in mud. Planted. He
touches my forehead.
I go limp. He turns into ocean. All falls
under a wash of blue.

The Lawsuit

They made claim and won all my livestock.
Fine. I never want to see another animal.
Heard they sold the goats to pay for topsoil.
Now they have the best yard in town—green
as a sea god's eyes. I walk by their place on
my way to buy lottery tickets. Staring at their
grass, I wish to drown in mowed shades
of rough waters.

Lottery Tickets

Cherry
            Cherry
                        Goat

Cherry
            Cherry
                        Goat

Cherry
            Hope
                        Goat

Hope
            Fuck
                        Goat

Circe Swallows Her Glass Eye

Setting is the lie; there is no physical ocean
keeping others from finding me. I live on
open farmland. There is little to do, so few
bother coming—though all roads overlap
at my door.

To fight the quiet, I talk to my selves, as
though we're sisters. This makes loneliness
lighter to carry from bed to kitchen, where
I make coffee and read past notes written
on top of the news.

It will be hot today. Like yesterday. Too
boring not to drift back to red lettering.
Zoophile, the paperboy has written, sure
that I won't call his boss

to complain. He's correct; I say nothing—
learned years ago, objection only invites
more lies. Truth is, I haven't had an animal
on the property—not since Odysseus left.

The Night Circe Cannot Remember

Drank too much. Bottle of ambrosia down
my own. Remember burning in a corner,
like a hand was striking matches on the back
of my throat. Remember a panhandler said
to me that night *drink has sunk more ships*
than Neptune ever will—sounded like a line
a man's taught to sing for someone else—
especially seeing how drunk the messenger
was—I ignored him and continued down.
Remember waking in a barn with a woman
screaming *with my goat*—the word *with*
sounding like a thing she was taught to say
instead of fuck. What she meant to say is
fucked my goat. I have no way of knowing
if I didn't—other than Penelope says I did.

AMBROSIA
- DRINK HAS SUNK MORE SHIPS
THAN NEPTUNE EVER WILL!

THE SAD SIREN

Book III: Voices across the Air

Within Circe, Something Goes Terribly Wrong

pulseisdrowningbreath

mustcutoffmyhandstoshallowthesea

Dear Odysseus,

I'm scared.

Normally my blood pressure is strangely low.
Even doctors comment on how I'd make
a great assassin, as my body hasn't the quiver
of a beat. The things people say scare me.
Last night I woke with a pain in my chest. It
felt as though three women ate of my heart;

each mouth moving distinctly. I knew them
as a mother knows the tug of her babe's suckle.
I haven't told anyone this; I'm afraid of what
people will say. I write to you, because you
refuse to speak to me. You should know, it
will cost me all my bread to have this message

delivered. Maybe knowing this will make my
words worth something. It is expensive to be
hated. Only hunger will consider handling
anything I touch. Before you, I could afford
more. I have a yellow hat, but wind has blown
the brim limp. I look like a flag with it on,

but I love the damn thing; it marks the last
time I could handle money with anonymity.
Now I am a million names I don't recognize. I
don't know my own story. Do you have it? If so,
I want it back. I do have a scrap of paper with
your signature—a letter closing with *Love.*

I will give you back this letter—will give all
the bread that sustains me—give my eyes—
my hat—that yellow flag of joy—for a reply.
Why my heart, when before it hadn't even
a quiver?

Hopefully,
Circe

The Postscript Circe Omits from Her Letter to Odysseus

P.S. The women in me have been telling
stories. They say you have my Odysseus—
that he is not a goat—my son is not a goat.
We have a son. You have our son. Give him
back. I want him back. Give him back.
Before we women take him.

Sea Nymphs with the Appetite of Birds

Longing for exotic curvatures, legs instead
of fins, they lasso with their arms, feet. Man
in hand they cry, *you come as promised, next to
me*. Rush of blood, warm scent turning soft
kisses into hard nibbles. With eye and nose
gone missing, seems best to keep eating until
tides bring another ship. Next chance, they'll
remember to be gentle—to take him without
consuming the veins that tie the heart to flesh.

The Sad Siren

The first man eaten, I loved more than myself. Every
bite taken of him, I bit two from my own flesh. But he
was formed of earth,
while I'm of motion. He diffused
as I grew to tidal. I attempted
to break my mouth on
the shore, only to
gather back as
a winged
fish. I
flew
towards
the sun to
be had by its
fire, but without
the cup of sea to drink
air from, I couldn't keep
conscious long enough to ignite.
With great effort he remained alive for
days. As I injured, so did I stitch the wounds with my
hair—bandaged gashes with seaweed.
But the scent of him would be
on my hands—I couldn't
think right
in its presence—hope
drunk,
would believe I
could lick
and survive
on taste
alone.

The Angry Siren

What my sad sister won't tell you
are the things the half-dead man
called her as she stitched his arms
back on—licking his toes to keep
herself from eating his face. I was

there to replant her teeth when she
bashed her jaw on shores. It was I
who cleaned ash from her scorched
skin. While she battled her nature, he
spat in her eyes and shat in her mouth—

yelling whore. She plucked out every
feather and stayed silent for ten days.
But inevitably, she remained air as he
turned to dirt. What was left of him fell
under sea—a sunken boat. She couldn't

help but resurface—rising as summer
night. Only now she sings only of him—
she is never present nor future—eyes
coated in spittle—the scent of him on
her tongue—gags me when she speaks.

She was all I had of home and he kicked
in and out her doors; for that loss I pro-
long every sailor's hurt for at least one
full night before swallowing pain like
cups of sugar at a sunrise feast of bones.

The Little Siren

The Sea
Witch gave
me the face of
a swordfish to impel
my sisters with. She says,
if I drink them I will grow feet
and lose my wings—then boys
will like me. But to do this I must
care nothing for sisters. I remain
silent with hopes that they
will forget me—that I
too will forget sisters,
before the sirens'
slaughter.

The Littlest Mermaid Reads Her Future from Her Imaginary Palm

This is the line where he would've
felt pulse when holding my hand.

In a Conversation between the Sad and Angry Sisters

I worry about our little siren—
she has made herself
a new set of hands
using shark's
teeth for
fingers.

The Littlest Siren Looks at Her Hands Made from Sharks' Teeth and Thinks

But they are my sisters.

THE
ANGRY
SIREN

The Little Siren

Book IV: *The Recipe for Sirens*

The Recipe for Sirens, Copyright Page

The Recipe for Sirens

The body is two doors hinged atop each
other, designed to swing
in opposite directions. To change someone,
enter from their back—
keyhole below left ribcage—tickles a bit—

unlocking. Inside, use a bird for a needle—
embroider the face
of starvation over the peephole, then exit
from the front. Surface
to a world where fish sprout wings and

appetites for harm; let them suck marrow
from a man's center—
drown them in fat. If they beg for mercy—
try to be patient—
most can't see you have already given them
what they ask for.

How to Turn Scream to Song

You must first teach your creature to breathe—in steps:

Hold the creature's teeth back with a
witch's eye.

For a lung, insert a paper lantern.

Then, sing into the creature's new
emptiness until it shines.

Uses for a Witch's Eye—1.a. Jaw Stopper

It's likely you are the only witch in territory,
meaning it's your own eye needed to
complete the spell. You

must resign yourself to this loss. Tell yourself
it's just an eye—you have two—and vision
happens regardless

of sight. It helps to find imperfections in
the victim socket—think *how weak the eye*
to let you ruin it. If you still cannot

bring yourself to harm, there are others who
will hurt you. Go to the local tavern—
offer to turn Anyman's goat into

a woman. He'll do whatever you ask to make
normal his love. Once you have your
prize, punish him for his offense.

Kill the goat—tell him—she was willingly his
before he required her to change. Leave
with a substance sufficient

to keep open a mouth. Now, you
are ready to feed your singing
want to Sirens.

How to Turn a Goat into a Woman

As editors, we are proud of this easy to perform, yet most effective, spell.

Here are the simple steps:

> Overnourish hope by feeding it a cold
> soup of tears.
>
> Shave off half its fur.
>
> Finally, don't question the results.

Uses for a Witch's Eye—1.b Jaw Stopper

Should you desire more
sight after the loss of
your least favorite eye,
may we suggest melting
a window into a marble—
wear the globe as a view
overlooking the ocean.

The Mother's Spell

Tell your creatures they came from your
womb; this is your best protection against
a fatal attack.

The recognition of a cage is inevitable. They
will hate you upon first sight of bars. They'll
eat your bones

to get at escape—unless they think of you
as origin.

Eliminating Your Creature Issues

Understand. No bookmarking parts—
no teeth, no hair, not a single feather—
burn the blue connecting cords. Read

the portrait of Odysseus carved into
your upper arm. Burn your arm.
Delight in the baritone sound of your

hand snapping with heat and pressure.
Cry for the girls, but know you can
make new creatures—the sea is full

of ceaseless want needing to be paid
a physical lesson. Hunger will soon
arrive at your door, again asking

to be punished with wings and song.

The Note Circe Skimmed Over

Now, not only will you enjoy the new harmonics of light, but you may also use this music as a reliable assessment of your creature's mental health. It is best to be preemptive with creature issues, as it is their faults that lead to your own demise.

On the Pages Not Self-Referenced, and Therefore Never Read, in *The Recipe for Sirens,* Odysseus Writes:

Circe, I'm sorry. I'm so sorry.

THE ANGRY SIREN

THE SAD SIREN

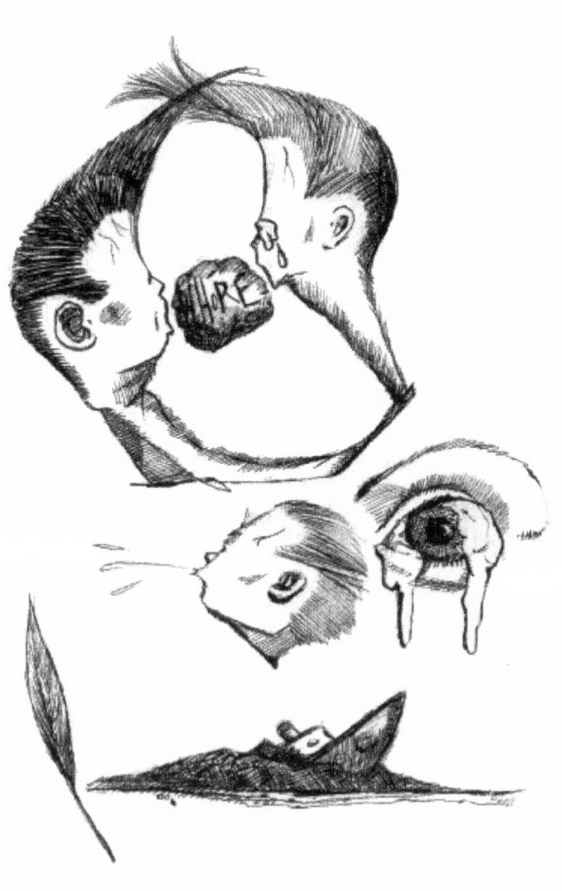
HOPE

Book V: Written in the Margins of *The Recipe for Sirens*

The Body Is Two Doors

For convenience, they had me birth you
in a common house—thin white walls
blocking sight, but not the sound of mouths
coming from wombs. I heard your first

cry, as though it were waves on a shore at
night—pitch black, but present. They took
you and left me with a rag full of ice—told
me to rest until I needn't rest. I refused to lie

down. Looking for you, I woke in a gutter
holding a goat. A joke. Blood on my thighs,
I walked home with the animal. With a knife
to the billy, I tried to bleed out the past—to

empty the memory of your elbow rolling
beneath me—I tried to forget how it felt
to be two doors hinged atop each other—
to be pulse upon pulse.

Sing into Empty until it Shines

It is cool. And I am tired.
Too tired to
start a fire, so I boil water.

If you were actually my
son, I would
not tell you such things—

but you are in the care of
another, so I tell
you everything. I met you

when I first saw your father.
Odd. Yes. But how
else to explain—I broke his

ribs with the ease of cracking
open an egg. Best
night of sex I ever had. And

then you were in me. Now
it all seems
so practical, but at the time

I had mistaken vulnerability
for love. Sometime
your dad would say he loved

me. I mistook his words for
a house, garden,
and the sound of your feet

down a hallway, frightened
by a storm,
your little self made quiet by

the heat under our family
quilt. I live all
of this, in my head. How

to tell you, *No one can know*
the extent of another's loss. I
stir my tea and hear your feet.

Vision Happens Regardless of Sight

Dear O, I've been told drink makes
truth froth from a soul's center.

When we first met you slurred
your words—said I had eyes
bright as birds—how you wanted
to hold flight.

I thought you were making a punch
line of me—how as a child a tree
branch stole my eye.

So, I handed you my glass globe
replacement and left. I never
expected you to follow after me—

knocking on my door with gifts
of return— explaining how you
loved to play marbles—entering

me with my eye in your palm—
seeing my face, not as a void,
but a window.

Eat Your Bones to Get at Escape

Penelope my sister
thank you
for loving our child
as we could
not love ourselves

sister my Penelope
you thank
child our loving for
could we as
ourselves love not

Connecting Cords

I never slept with a goat.
I slept with another woman's husband—
I hurt her.
I didn't mean to.
I thought
I loved him.
I thought love would swallow pain.
I was stupid.
I lost my son.
I was so stupid.
I am not stupid.
I am sad.
I am a sad story.
I don't like this story.
I'm going to rewrite it.
I don't think you'll be in the revision, but
I want you to know how grateful I am that
you were in this vision—
my accidental friend—
my imagined ocean—
We're getting closer to the shores of kindness.

Goat Woman

Why is hope a cold soup?

Why must we shave our warm fur to be
human?

Why this result? Why not another solution?
Why not why?

VISION HAPPENS REGARDLESS OF SIGHT

ABSINTHE

Book VI: Denouement

On the Day Circe Didn't Kill Penelope

I walk twelve miles with a rock in each
hand. When I arrive at their front gate,
Penelope and my Odysseus are playing
in the grass. On her back, she lifts him
with her feet into the air—he spreads his
hands above her as though he is flying.
He looks like a god. I believe in gods
again. He laughs and a strand of drool
falls from his chin and lands on her chest—
it looks as though light itself sews the two
of them together—I think—this is how I
would have loved him. With a rock in each,
I leave without them knowing I ever came.

Circe upon Seeing Her Lost Son, Believes in (and Questions the) Gods Again

What can one do with Gods,
other than write them? Burn

the page and have ink turn
to smoke—its dark curves

streaming upward—sirens.
Smoke is how sorrow moves—

dry currents on my wet shores.
But do Gods ache with imagination?

Do they,

like us, draw into themselves, fire
at the final strokes of burning?

I will waste every match in my house to find
out—if Gods breathe, I will singe every hem
on Olympus with my efforts.

The Sirens in Circe

Sirens have been taking hammers to my glass
eye—crab shells strapped to a sailor's femur.
The leverage of living arms and a dead leg
against my back vision. What was a man is
now fractured flesh—periscope of
skin and blue motion. Perhaps I'm watching
him put on his pants? Perhaps leaving, when
broken into glass shards, resembles the ocean?

The Message Found in a Half-Burned Letter to Nyx

Skin-winged Nyx, some say…

…your eggs lay in the external wombs of shadows…

...my son is beyond my light…

…day and night
contract at the line of you…

…witches know…

all is done in one rotation—every rising is a
falling—

…what is done by day is undone by night…

…I could have been a Penelope, if not for
Penelope…

…to be visibly invisible…

…to be Penelope, for one
day…

I have cut out half my tongue as a gift for you.
Please. Oh God. Please…one day.

Circe Wakes as Penelope

Odysseus does not come to bed—spends his
nights looking at jars; gestures of a hand job
from topless sirens. The image poorly drawn,

has their fingers resemble weapons. He will
sleep when we rise. I've learned to treasure his
distance—gives room in our bed for a child.

I watch my son on the brink of waking—his
whole tumbling in waves of breath—without
muscles to mask the mechanics of life, his

face pulses. Oh, this is love for the loveless. I no
longer feel like I am waiting. As a witness, I am
alive—even if my husband thinks of me as death.

Circe Teaches Her Son How to Fish

Cut my hand gutting a trout—slight incision,
but substantial color. Suck my own
wound and continue up the trout's belly. Its
silver body instructing the knife
to stop where gills connect—tough joint—
place where escape once lived. On
the ground, this animal's interior spreads like
violet paint across rocks. My red
runs through intestines towards a river bank.
My chance to diffuse in currents
disappears with the sun's dry tongue—lapping
this fish and my injury up into
its mouth. This event peels and appears
as an unfinished map drawn on
stone—an illustration missing destination. I
should have been more mindful—
should have arranged this death as an artist—
revered it like the god of wetness—
with rain beckoning return to fish and slits.
Should have carried it all
off to the never finished canvas of the sea.

Circe Wakes as Herself after Being Penelope

There is never enough time to teach the art of return.
Home is the lie that never stops telling stories. Once

upon a time there were three sisters. Sirens who tried
to love everything they were not. They failed

and kept failing until a ship sailed past their efforts.
They burst into sea foam—followed the men to shore.

The salt of their arms made it onto the men's tables.
They were no longer monsters, but flavor. Sorrow

can be delicious. Son, enjoy sadness, but don't live
there. This is only a story. The sisters will find their

way back to the sea and I'll always be a sort of home—
even if home is a lie telling stories.

Tonya
THE SAD SIREN

Book VII: Postscript

Today I took a fishing-hook and unlaced
the stitch-work on my arms.
When the doctor comes, I will remember
everything. If my son comes,
I will tell him I remember everything.

Should no one come, I have written
over the Book of Spells *what I know:*
Love cannot be translated, and yet
it is the only thing worth knowing.

A Reader's Epilogue

Page one. Again.

So they sent their ravishing voices out
across the air and the heart inside me
throbbed to listen longer.

—Odysseus, *The Odyssey*

Acknowledgments

The author is grateful to the following journals where the poems have previously appeared, sometimes in a different form.

Ampersand Review, blossombones, Contrary, Entasis, Hot Metal Bridge, Inlandia Institute, Off the Coast, Paper Darts, The Pedestal Magazine, Requited, Rougarou, Saturation, and *Verdad,*

The ebb and flow of this book would not exist without the editorial eye of Adam Smith.

Thank you Alexis Vergalla, Cheryl Gross, Karl Preusser, and John Michalski for contributing paint, motion, and sound.

Matt Ryan, you are a wonderful editor. Thank you for turning words into artifacts. Thank you for Lowbrow books.

Great Thanks (N.D.)

JJ Davis, Curtis Thornhill, Mom, Dad, Little Jon, Stan, Chris, and my gracious family.

Charles Hood, Dani Keinz, Mark Hoffer, Melanie Jeffrey, Rachel Jennings, Santi Tafarella, M.M. McGuire, and the rest of my AVC family.

Charles MacQuarrie, Steven Frye, and my CSUB family.

Juan Felipe Herrera, Maurya Simon, Chris Abani, Susan Straight, Goldberry Long, Chris Buckley, Stephanie Hammer, Laila Lalami, and my UCR family.

My dear friends Kate Preusser, Curt Hanson, J. Hernandez, Sarahbell Foster, Grace and Ryan Franz.

My Glass Family (thank you Ron).

Kate Gale, Mark Cull, Alma Mckertich, Natasha Saje, Dawn Potter, Roxane Gay, Jason Cook, Colin Meldrum, Cody Todd, Kaitlin Hillenbrand, Ken Robidoux, Matt Mauch, Peter Schwartz, J. Shiok, and my writing families.

Great Thanks (C.G.)

Louis, Katina, Lucille, the Toms, Janice, Christine, Kathleen, Jenny, Sandy, Joe, Kathleen, and Harley.

About the Author

Originally from Utah, Nicelle Davis now resides in Quartz Hill, California, with her son J.J. She teaches at Antelope Valley College. She is managing editor of Colibrí Press. Her book, *Becoming Judas*, is forthcoming from Red Hen Press in 2013 and *In the Circus of You* (a collaboration with Cheryl Gross) is forthcoming from Rose Metal Press in 2014.

Photo by John Michalski

About the Illustrator

Born and raised in Brooklyn, Cheryl Gross started her career as an illustrator and painter. Her work has appeared in galleries and museums throughout the world, including Laforet Harajuku Museum in Japan, The Brooklyn Museum, and The Museum of the City of New York. Cheryl is an Adjunct Professor in the Communications Design Department at Pratt Institute, where she teaches illustration and motion graphics. She is also a Visiting Instructor at Bloomfield College in New Jersey.

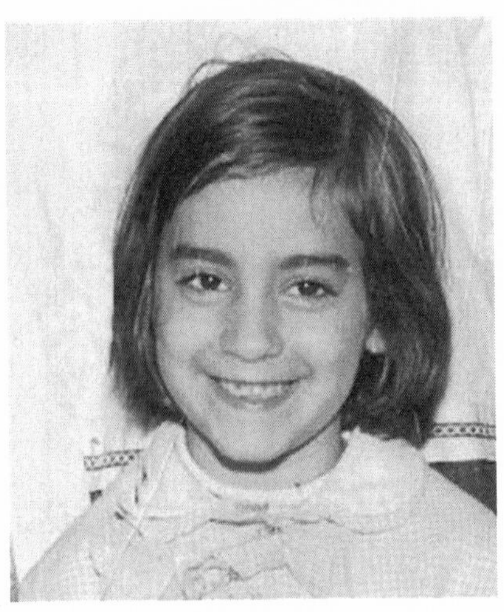

Self-Portrait

17479697R00062

Printed in Great Britain
by Amazon